Thanku
POEMS OF GRATITUDE

신선영 Sun Yung Shin   Padma Venkatraman   Charles Waters   Naomi Shihab Nye

Becky Shillington   Janice Scully   Jane Yolen

Kimberly Blaeser   Ed DeGaria   Gwendolyn Hooks   Carole Lindstrom   Baptiste Paul

Joseph Bruchac   Sarvinder Naberhaus   Cynthia Leitich Smith

Sylvia Liu   Patti Richards   Lupe Ruiz-Flores   Margarita Engle

Carolyn Dee Flores   Chrystal D. Giles   Kenn Nesbitt   Megan Hoyt

Diana Murray   Renée M. LaTulippe   Charles Ghigna

JaNay Brown-Wood   Jamie McGillen   Edna Cabcabin Moran

Liz Garton Scanlon   Traci Sorell

Vanessa Brantley-Newton

Illustrated by **MARLENA MYLES**

Edited by **MIRANDA PAUL**

M Millbrook Press • Minneapolis

For Lucille Clifton, Kaia Sand, Michael Glaser, Lisa Moser, and Linda Vander Heyden—thank you for shaping my writer's journey. And to my friends, cofounders, and team members at We Need Diverse Books—my family is forever grateful for your advocacy, passion, and persistence.
—M.P.

Thank you to the little seeds that bloom into the many vibrant colors that inspire my art and give it purpose
—M.M.

Millbrook Press™
An imprint of Lerner Publishing Group, Inc.
241 First Avenue North
Minneapolis, MN 55401 USA

For reading levels and more information, look up this title at www.lernerbooks.com.

Designed by Danielle Carnito and Viet Chu.
Main body text set in Mikado Regular.
Typeface provided by HVD fonts.
The illustrations in this book were created in Adobe Illustrator with Texturino.

Library of Congress Cataloging-in-Publication Data

The Cataloging-in-Publication Data for *Thanku: Poems of Gratitude* is on file at the Library of Congress.
ISBN 978-1-5415-2363-0 (lib. bdg.)
ISBN 978-1-5415-6100-7 (eb pdf)

Manufactured in the United States of America
1-44487-34695-2/25/2019

Giving Thanks

by Joseph Bruchac
In memory of Chief Jake Swamp

Thanksgiving is more
than just one day,
so a Mohawk elder
said to me.

Though it is good
that we remember
this time with feasting
each November.

We need to give thanks
every dawn
for the gifts of life,
for each breath drawn.

For everything
that keeps us living,
we speak our words
of true thanksgiving.

format: didactic poem

Dear Sky

by Naomi Shihab Nye

Dear Sky,

Thank you for sticking around.
I'm a little trapped here, tied to ground by gravity,
in a state, a country, but you
are the true top of my room.
When I stare up, everything feels better.
You calm me down. When you are gray, I know you
are holding on to rain, doing your job. When you're blue,
everyone loves you. So many styles of clouds
drifting quietly . . . best of all, you always change,
the way I change getting older.
Thank you for showing me how. In your own
mysterious way, I think you care. I want to belong
to everywhere, the way you do. Kids in Dubai,
Kenya, China, Australia, all know you.
You are the true world friend. Sky, I thank you
every day and night for connecting us.
I don't need any money at all
to own your glory.

Love, Small Dot on the Earth

format: epistle

Flights

by Kimberly Blaeser

Do
flying birds
feel gratitude to air,
to curved and feathered tips of wings?
Their sky colors wave like flags in wind: canary yellow, cardinal red, crow black, or flamingo pink.
Rainbow bird wings flex then lift **up up up up**. Strong wings bend, push **down down down down.**
Like kites, birds whirl and dip and dive in a high curving dance—but with no strings to earth!
Sometimes their down flap is like a clap, their glide is like a **wheeee**.
Some days the skies seem full of **honk** and **tweet** and **chirp**,
seem full of **caw** and **chick-a-dee-dee-dee.**
And when the landing bird
s-p-r-e-a-d-s its fancy feather fan,
our hearts may clap in gratitude at that.
Returning to earth, does a landing bird give thanks
for its amazing steering rudder, the balance of its sturdy tail?
Do we earthbound watchers who only dream of feathered flight
sigh thanks to nature's aerial artists—who lift us imaginatively on their wings?

format: concrete (shape)

Dinosaur

by 신선영 Sun Yung Shin

You stand, not like a ghost but a cage and crown of bones—
my skull, ribs, hips, and knees thank you for showing me how to be proud
to dream of a feathered future; we will swim in the sky.

format: sijo

Constellation
by Ed DeCaria

To
think
gene-sized
mutations
spawned generations
of such stunning variations!
Marvelous, this evolving human constellation . . .

format: Fib

Appreciation Equations
by Becky Shillington

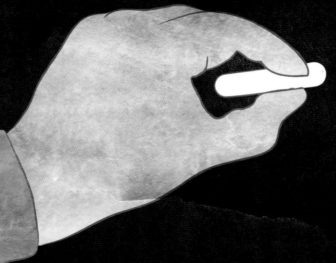

(family + friends) + love = a thankful heart

KINDNESS$^\infty$ = A BETTER WORLD

$\dfrac{\text{HOPE}}{\text{hello}}$ = NEW KID

$$\dfrac{\text{MOUNTAINS} + \text{TREES} + \text{OCEANS} + \text{SUN}}{\text{nature's gifts}} = \text{4 every 1}$$

format: math poems

Nothing to Be Grateful For

by Padma Venkatraman

Indians drew me.
Arabs grew me. Without me,
you'd have no rockets,
no laptops, no phones. Zero:
With me, came a whole new world.

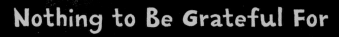

format: tanka

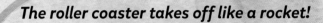

The Best Birthday Present: A Poem for Two Voices

by Gwendolyn Hooks

I asked Mom for a Fun City birthday party.

I asked Mom for a Beach Blast birthday party.

I asked Mom for a Rock the Wall birthday party.

But Mom said, "You can have a party at home."
Who wants a homemade birthday party?

Never?

Your birthday is two weeks after mine.
We'll have one party for the both of us!

I'll have to ask, but she'll say yes
if your mom says yes.

Fingers crossed. Thank you.

The roller coaster takes off like a rocket!

Surf's up!

We'll reach the highest mountain peak!

Me. I've never had a birthday party.

Never.

We will?

Fingers crossed.

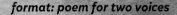

format: poem for two voices

The Race of Friends

by Jane Yolen

Better than a thank-you is
a grateful child who takes up
wand, then races on around

that far bend, handing off the
gift of wand at race's end
to another need-filled friend.

format: septercet

First Responder

by Janice Scully

Like an ambulance on my desk,

waiting to fix a torn page

or a broken book.

At my service,

armored helper,

cradling a bold, circular

heart, ready

for any emergency,

holding still

for the yank

and the quick rip

of a smooth piece that will

save a poem, a story,

or an injured photograph.

You park nearby,

ready to

help again.

format: hyperbole

Roy G. Biv
by Charles Waters

Roy G. Biv has lots to give
during a waterfall,
kaleidoscopes of color,
a rainbow for us all.

format: quatrain

Drops of Gratitude

by Carole Lindstrom

rain

fell   water

dripped from

the

roof

drips

thumped.   dust

gritty

drops

insects

greet the

rain,

format: found poem

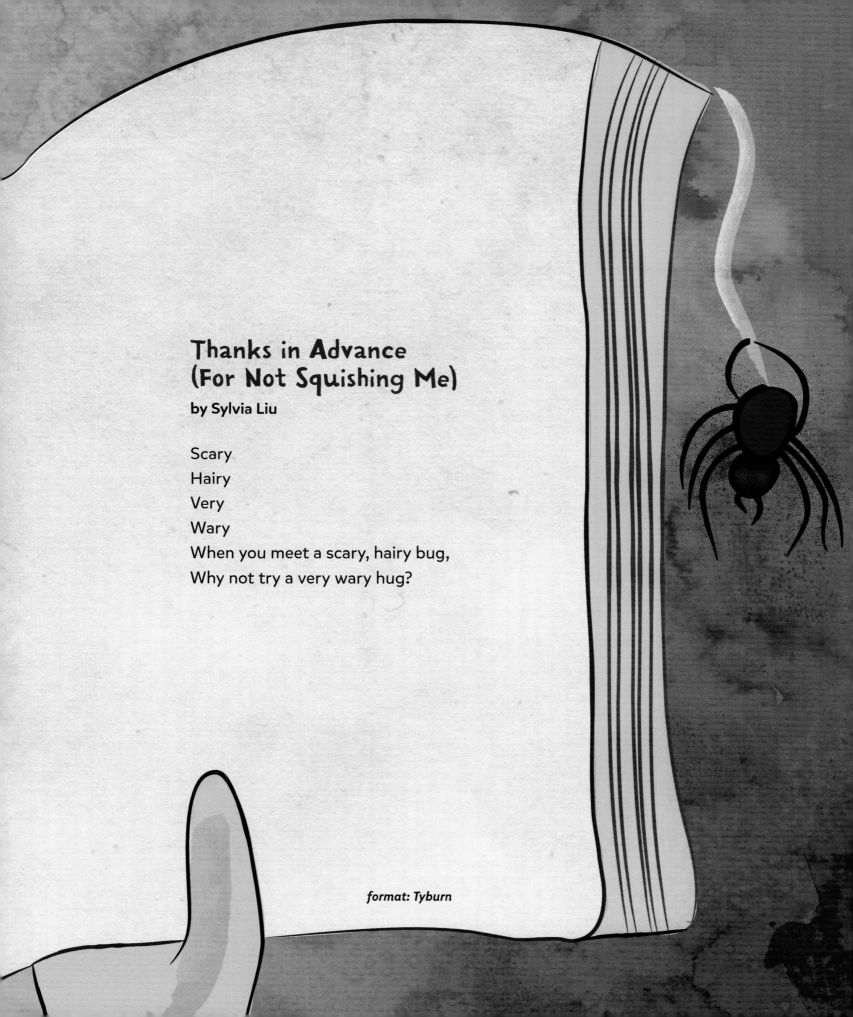

Thanks in Advance
(For Not Squishing Me)

by Sylvia Liu

Scary

Hairy

Very

Wary

When you meet a scary, hairy bug,

Why not try a very wary hug?

format: Tyburn

Thank You, Sleep!

by Carolyn Dee Flores

A-choo!
Boo-hoo!
Coughing, creeping, drippy, eww.
Flush, gunk, hic. I'm sunk.
Onomatopoeia-*choo*!

Itchy, jitter, knocking knees,
L-m-n-o-pia ooze. (Oh, please.)
Quite sick. Queasy—quick!
Onomatopoeia-*ick*!

Ringing in my ears and head.
Slurping soup, I jump in bed.
Ticktock, ticktock, snooze and snore . . .

Thank you, Sleep! I'm sick no more.

Farewell, Sneeze. Bye, Bellyache.
I feel great. Now, I'm awake!
Ultra-Vultra, whoosh and whoom,
Out the door to play: *X-Y-Zoom*!

format: onomatopoeia

Atta-Dude

by Sarvinder Naberhaus

Sorry where your life sits?

    Pits

A sad pill to swallow?

    Wallow

Disguised as something pretty?

    Pity

Singing the Poor Me blues?

    Lose

Choosing melancholy?

    Folly

Maybe change your attitude

    Gratitude

Give yourself some latitude

    Atta-dude

The clouds will go away

    Say

All you're thankful for

    Score!

format: echo

No More Holes for Broken Soles

by Lupe Ruiz-Flores

Shoes, shoes, shoes.
Lined up neatly on shelves
brown ones, black ones, white ones,
sharing a common bond—
all used.

Shoes, shoes, shoes.
Boots, heels, sandals, sneakers,
broken, scuffed, and torn—
all crying out for attention.

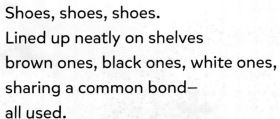

Shoes, shoes, shoes.
A cobbler starts to repair them,
tapping, sewing, polishing—
making them useful again.

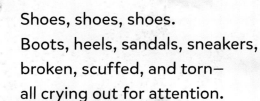

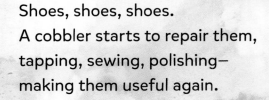

format: allegory

Each Scar

by Baptiste Paul

My mom says
be thankful
for each scar.

So I play.
Fail each day.
Lose my way.

Bash, crash, rough—
Mom, it's tough
to thank scars.

format: tricube

Stories for Dinner

by Cynthia Leitich Smith

Round the feast-day table, we say Grace and Talk Story,
sharing turkey, potatoes, cranberries, casseroles.

I hear tell of a Blackfoot great-grandfather, son of a minister.
He carves animals from wood with his pocketknife.

I hear tell of a Muscogee great-granddad, boarding-school captive,
how he flew over the Pacific to defend our homeland.

I hear tell of his big sister, raised in that same school,
owned a grocery, spoke English, Spanish, and Mvskoke.

I hear tell of her nephew, who patched war wounds in the jungle,
stomp danced in a circle, steered eighteen-wheelers down highways.

I hear tell of his sister, my grandma, who cooked this dinner.
Marched for Water Protectors. Wears a "Native Pride" T-shirt.

I hear tell of her daughter, my mama, who studied nursing.
She and my architect daddy fell in love junior year at college.

I hear tell of everyday heroes. Some passed on, others right here.
How they prayed and planned for future generations, for me.

Here come the pecan pies, fresh and warm from the oven,
with laughter, love, gratitude, sweet iced cream.

Here come more stories, ones I'll retell someday
around another feast-day table of faith, food, friends, and family.

format: chant, free verse

Alice Thanks the Looking Glass(es)

by Patti Richards

I'm here to get my glasses,
'Cause things are kind of blurry.
Grandma says, "Be thankful,
They'll look perfect, not to worry."

The doctor takes them out.
"No peeking. Count to three.
Now, Alice, look around the room
And tell me what you see."

I see Grandma's Cheshire smile,
And letters on the wall—
The big *G* on the top and the
Y that's very small!

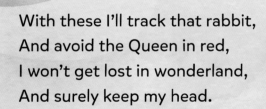

With these I'll track that rabbit,
And avoid the Queen in red,
I won't get lost in wonderland,
And surely keep my head.

I'm grateful for my spectacles
And what they help me see.
But most of all, I'm quite obliged
Behind them, I'm still me.

format: narrative poem, allusion

Dimples

by Chrystal D. Giles

Deep indents in my brown skin
Inspired by the smile bouncing upward from my toes
Mirror to the brightness in my soul
Pools of laughter, bubbling up and spilling out
Love, light, and bursts of cheer
Expressions of peace, pops of joy
Sun-soaked, beaming cheeks, reflections of happy me

format: acrostic

I'm Thankful for My Puppy

by Margarita Engle

I'm grateful for the bouncy way
your four legs lead me on a race
at this wild, impossible pace
that invites me to run, leap, play!

I can't imagine a whole day
of dull commands like down, sit, stay.

I love the colorful array
of trees and birds in each new place,
as your swift legs lead the footrace
back home to our restful doorway.

format: décima mirror

I Picked up a Wallet

by Kenn Nesbitt

Just yesterday morning,
I picked up a wallet
that someone had dropped
by mistake on the street.

By mailing it back to
the person who lost it
I made us both happier.
Isn't that neat?

FRAGILE

format: McWhirtle

Falling Leaves

by JaNay Brown-Wood

I loved the leaves
That dropped from the trees
And danced in the breeze
In Autumn.

The vibrant reds
That fell on my head
Or the lawn where I tread
And trot on 'em.

And all around
Shades of yellow and brown
Flit-flew to the ground
As I caught 'em!

A special thank-you
To the trees that grew
The wind that blew
My hands that threw
And my heart that knew 'em
In Autumn.

format: ode

Diary of a Sweatshirt: The Best Day Ever

by Diana Murray

Today I felt a lovely breeze while playing in the leaves.
I got a little dirty, though, especially my sleeves.
My pockets got filled up with rocks, which surely was no pleasure.
And yet, I must admit, it's awfully fun to dig for treasure.
I snagged my fabric on a branch while climbing up a tree.
But, oh! What an amazing view. I've never felt so free!
I'm used to being in my drawer, all neatly tucked away.
I'm thankful I got worn for once, outside where I could play.

format: mask

Thanksgiving at the Lake

by Megan Hoyt

I walk beside the icy lake and spot
A duckling, camouflaged beneath the reeds,
Along the distant edge, a tiny dot—
His papa—gathers food among the weeds.
I wonder, will he slide on wobbly legs,
With mushed-up worms and crunchy little bugs,
While Mama gently warms her other eggs,
To feed his son and give him duckling hugs?
My daddy's hauling fishing nets onboard
His breath a cloud, he stands on aching feet.
He swings the sail and grasps the heavy cord,
I watch him, twirling, from the captain's seat.
A busy father's work is never done,
from daylight's birth until the setting sun.

format: Shakespearean sonnet

The Perfect Rock

by **Jamie McGillen**

Beside the ocean, blue as me,
I saw an egg-shaped rock.
I don't know why it winked at me
to interrupt my walk.

All slippery and black as coal,
it fit right in my hand.
My lonely frown fell down a hole
forever lost in sand.

It nestled in my little fist,
the smoothest, kindest stone.
I can't believe I almost missed
this treasure of my own.

I squeezed it tight and made a wish.
I almost threw it back,
where foamy waves and scaly fish
could swallow or attack.

Instead, I held it to my cheek,
my perfect ocean rock.
I'm grateful that it winked at me
and chose me on that walk.

format: ballad

Autumn by the Sea

by Renée M. LaTulippe

Tuscany, Italy

Autumn falls softly by the sea:
sunset wears her cinnamon blush,
rockrose beckons a lingering bee—
we wrap ourselves in a comfortable hush.

A sunset wearing cinnamon blush
traces shapes on brown-gold sand,
wraps us in a comfortable hush
as we amble in our wonderland.

Tracing shapes on brown-gold sand,
lazy waves fall back, then swell.
We amble in our wonderland,
etching thanks with stick and shell.

Lazy waves fall back, then swell,
rockrose beckons a lingering bee.
We etch our thanks with stick and shell
as Autumn falls softly by the sea.

format: pantoum

Thankful for Thinking

by Vanessa Brantley-Newton

There's no telling the places our brains can take us
Or ways in which our thoughts can shape us—
Smart and happy or creative,
Brave, elated, innovative,
There's no telling the people our ***dreams*** will make us!

format: limerick

College Degree

by Traci Sorell

The first.
First diploma.
Family proud, new life.
Opportunities everywhere.
Grateful.

format: cinquain

A Graceful Journey

by Edna Cabcabin Moran

Keep on paddling
Any place you want to go.
You steer yourself
Any place you want to go.
Keep on paddling.

format: palindrome

Paint the Sunset

by Charles Ghigna

Paint the sunset with your eyes,
Sculpt the morning with your heart,
Brush your dreams with light and laughter,
Make your life a work of art.

format: metaphor

All This
by Liz Garton Scanlon

Snow
a book
hot cocoa
a bubble bath
and two curled-up cats.
Another book, more snow
and those cats—oh, how they purr.
Even when the world's dark and cold
there is all this to be grateful for
and I purr too: ***Thank you, thank you, thank you.***

format: Etheree

Poetic Forms and Literary Devices   (Please Try These at Home!)

When reading *Thanku: Poems of Gratitude*, you might notice a diversity of poetic forms. No two poems in this collection follow the same structure, just as no two humans are exactly alike. This book was intentionally designed to showcase a range of well-known and lesser-known styles of poems, including some formats that were recently invented. Here's more about them:

A **didactic poem** usually includes a clear message or lesson that readers can take away from it. What do you think the message is in Joseph Bruchac's poem "Giving Thanks"?

Epistle is another word for a letter. Do you think the speaker in Naomi Shihab Nye's "Dear Sky" will send her letter via airmail?

Concrete poems (also called shape poems) use special arrangements or typeface to create visual effects that match the topic. What shape do you see in Kimberly Blaeser's poem "Flights"?

The Korean traditional poem known as **sijo** contains three lines of 14–16 syllables. Some sijo poems cover deep questions, knowledge, or abstract thoughts. What does your knowledge about dinosaurs and humans lead you to understand about the poem "Dinosaur" by 신선영 Sun Yung Shin?

Fibonacci poetry (nicknamed **Fib**) is a new form founded by children's author and poet Gregory K. Pincus. It is inspired by a mathematical sequence of the same name, where each line has a specific number of syllables. Ed DeCaria's poem "Constellation" includes seven lines with the following number of syllables in each: 1, 1, 2, 3, 5, 8, 13. Reading it is kind of like counting stars, only much easier.

Math poems incorporate numbers, equations, or math symbols with words to create meanings or express ideas. Would you prefer doing the homework included in Becky Shillington's "Appreciation Equations" or your regular schoolwork?

A **tanka** is a five-line, traditional Japanese poem containing lines of 5 or 7 syllables, with 31 syllables total. Tanka poems often give a complete picture of a mood or of a historical event. What long-ago invention fuels Padma Venkatraman's poem "Nothing to Be Grateful For"?

Poems for two voices sound like conversation or dialogue when read aloud because they are written for two people to perform. In Gwendolyn Hooks's poem "The Best Birthday Present: A Poem for Two Voices," can you see how the conversation goes back and forth on the page, with each speaker's words on one side?

The **septercet**, invented by Jane Yolen, is a poem that may or may not rhyme. Verses are in three lines (like the tercet), but each line has 7 syllables—from the Latin word *septem* (seven).

Hyperbole is an overexaggeration that can create emphasis or humor but is meant figuratively—not to be taken as true in the literal sense. In Janice Scully's poem, what object is being compared to a "First Responder" that rushes to help in a time of crisis?

A **quatrain** is a four-line stanza or poem, and the lines often alternate rhymes just as in Charles Waters's colorful poem "Roy G. Biv."

Found poetry means taking outside sources—magazines, newspapers, signs, or other written material—and making a new poem out of bits and pieces from them, much like a collage. Carole Lindstrom's poem "Drops of Gratitude" was created using words from the page of a book.

A **Tyburn** poem has six lines. The first four lines each have a single 2-syllable rhyming word. Line five has 9 syllables, and syllables 5 through 8 are the words from lines one and two. Line six likewise has 9 syllables, and syllables 5 through 8 are the words from lines three and four. Historically, these poems protested executions. Will you spare the bug in Sylvia Liu's "Thanks in Advance (For Not Squishing Me)"?

Onomatopoeia is forming words based on sound effects, and sometimes these are nonsense words that express emotions or actions. Carolyn Dee Flores's poem "Thank You, Sleep!" is filled with onomatopoeia, many of which appear in alphabetical order.

In an **echo poem**, the last word or syllable of a line is echoed underneath to form a rhyming line. When you read "Atta-Dude" by Sarvinder Naberhaus, one person reads a line, then the group calls out the echo!

An **allegory** is writing that contains fictional figures or symbols meant to represent real people or big ideas. In Lupe Ruiz-Flores's poem "No More Holes for Broken Soles," who might the worn-out shoes represent? How about the helpful cobbler?

A **tricube** includes three stanzas, each with three lines, and each line has 3 syllables. Can you count three beats in every line of "Each Scar" by Baptiste Paul?

A **chant** simply includes repeating lines or phrases and may be one of poetry's oldest forms. Cynthia Leitich Smith's poem "Stories for Dinner" uses a repeating chant, while the rest is written in **prose** (ordinary language) and **free verse** (nonstructured) couplets.

A **narrative** poem tells a story and often is written in the voice of the main character. Patti Richards's poem "Alice Thanks the Looking Glass(es)" also makes **allusions** (quick mentions or references) to a well-known story and its characters. Don't fall asleep, or you might miss them!

In an **acrostic**, the first (or last) letters of a line spell out a word or phrase. Sometimes, like in Chrystal D. Giles's poem "Dimples," the title is the same as what the letters spell.

The **décima mirror** is a traditional Cuban poetry form consisting of two redondillas (8-syllable quatrains) with a couplet (two-line) bridge, in the following rhyme pattern: *abba aa abba*. Can you feel the beats bounce during the playful walk of "I'm Thankful for My Puppy" by Margarita Engle?

American poet Bruce Newling invented the **McWhirtle**, which, according to Kenn Nesbitt, "is basically a double-dactyl without the requirements for a 6-syllable word or a higgledy-piggledy nonsense phrase." In other words, it's a difficult form made simple—like the complex ideas of responsibility and karma easily explained within the scenario of returning someone's wallet.

An **ode** is a poem that praises or celebrates someone or something. Historically, many odes were meant to be sung. Can you hear a rhythm in JaNay Brown-Wood's poem "Falling Leaves"?

A **mask** (also called persona) is a poem written from the point of view of an object or animal. Sometimes mask poems feel like riddles because the speaker's identity isn't stated. If you covered up the title "Diary of a Sweatshirt: The Best Day Ever" in Diana Murray's poem, what clues would help someone guess who or what is speaking?

Most **sonnets** have fourteen lines, with 10 syllables per line and a set pattern of rhyme. Megan Hoyt's poem "Thanksgiving at the Lake" follows the Shakespearean style of sonnet, where the last couplet (two lines) reveals an idea or conclusion.

A **ballad** is a poem or song that tells a story with short lines. Many ballads, like Jamie McGillen's "The Perfect Rock," have simple rhymes and a repeating rhythm that can be danced to or clapped out.

A **pantoum** is not an easy poem to write! This Malay verse form, which became popular in Britain and France in the 1800s, has a set pattern of how to repeat specific lines. In Renée M. LaTulippe's poem "Autumn by the Sea," the repeating lines mirror the movement of waves that continue to lap against the shore. Can you hear the pattern?

A **limerick** is a single verse with three long lines and two short lines, in the rhyme scheme of *aabba*. Said to be inspired by the Irish town of Limerick, these poems often make people smile or laugh. What made you smile while reading "Thankful for Thinking" by Vanessa Brantley-Newton?

An unrhymed **cinquain** (also known as a quintet) is a five-line poem, such as Traci Sorell's "College Degree."

A **palindrome** is a word, phrase, verse, sentence, or even poem that reads the same forward or backward. Edna Cabcabin Moran's poem "A Graceful Journey" can be read from the first to the last line or the last to the first, but can you spot the other palindrome?

A **metaphor** is a figure of speech that describes a thing by calling it something else that it couldn't possibly be in real life. In Charles Ghigna's poem "Paint the Sunset," the final line compares our lives with works of art. What will yours look like?

An **Etheree** is a ten-line unrhymed poem that begins with a 1-syllable line, and lines "grow" by 1 syllable in each line after. In Liz Garton Scanlon's poem "All This," the single, chilly word *snow* opens the poem, and it ends with a warm and cozy final image.

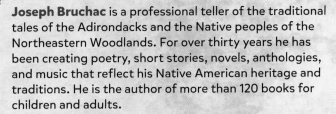

People to Be Grateful For (Also known as contributors to this book)

Joseph Bruchac is a professional teller of the traditional tales of the Adirondacks and the Native peoples of the Northeastern Woodlands. For over thirty years he has been creating poetry, short stories, novels, anthologies, and music that reflect his Native American heritage and traditions. He is the author of more than 120 books for children and adults.

Naomi Shihab Nye is a poet and anthologist and the acclaimed author of *The Turtle of Oman* and *Sitti's Secrets*, a picture book, based on her own experiences visiting her beloved Sitti in Palestine. She has taught writing and worked in schools all over the world. She lives in San Antonio, Texas.

Kimberly Blaeser is Anishinaabe and an enrolled member of the Minnesota Chippewa Tribe. She grew up on the White Earth Reservation. She was selected to serve as Wisconsin Poet Laureate in 2015–2016. Currently, she is a professor of creative writing and Native American literatures, and she is working on a collection of "Picto-Poems" that combines her photographs and poetry.

신선영 Sun Yung Shin was born in Seoul, Korea, and grew up in the Chicago area. She is a poet, editor, and the author of *Cooper's Lesson*, a bilingual illustrated book for children. She currently lives in Minneapolis where she codirects the community organization Poetry Asylum with poet Su Hwang.

Ed DeCaria is a kids' author and creator of the Madness! Poetry tournament. He continually experiments with ways to fuse traditional publishing with new technologies to help kids and teens more easily connect with poetry in their schools, homes, and lives.

Becky Shillington's first publication was in the local newspaper when she was in second grade. She's lived in Florida, North Carolina, Texas, and South Carolina. When not writing, she enjoys reading, playing the piano, hiking, and camping.

Padma Venkatraman is an American writer and oceanographer who has lived in five countries. In her line of work she has explored rain forests, played with mathematics, and served as chief scientist on research vessels. She now shares the sea of stories within her through her books.

Gwendolyn Hooks is the author of twenty books for children. She writes both fiction and nonfiction to encourage children to explore their world. Readers will find pets, friendship, and family sprinkled throughout Hooks's stories because that's what inspires her. She currently lives in Oklahoma City, Oklahoma.

Jane Yolen is an author of children's books, fantasy, and science fiction, including *Owl Moon*, *The Devil's Arithmetic*, and *How Do Dinosaurs Say Goodnight?* She is also a poet, a teacher of writing and literature, and a reviewer of children's literature.

Janice Scully is a graduate of the Vermont College MFA program in writing for children and young adults. Her writing has been published in *Highlights*, *Boston Literary Magazine*, and the Syracuse Poster Project. She currently resides in Fayetteville, New York.

Charles Waters was born in Philadelphia and raised in a nearby suburb. After graduating from Fairleigh Dickinson University, he joined several theater touring companies and spent eight years as an actor for Walt Disney World. He is the coauthor of *Can I Touch Your Hair? Poems of Race, Mistakes, and Friendship*.

Carole Lindstrom is the author of *Girls Dance, Boys Fiddle*, inspired by the fiddle's importance to her Metis culture. Lindstrom is Metis/Ojibwe and is tribally enrolled with the Turtle Mountain Band of Chippewa Indians. She was born and raised in Nebraska and currently makes her home in Maryland, where she's hard at work on a young adult novel.

Sylvia Liu made art growing up in Venezuela and continued to find creative outlets while working in environmental law. She now spends her days painting, writing, and drawing for kids and running KidLit411, a resource for authors and illustrators. Her debut picture book, *A Morning with Grandpa*, was a 2013 New Voices Award Winner from Lee & Low Books.

Carolyn Dee Flores grew up traveling around the world, thanks to an air force dad. Before coming back to illustration (the thing she loved the most), Flores was a professional rock musician and composer who wrote soundtracks for television and film. She is now hard at work on her eighth book for children and lives in San Antonio, Texas.

Sarvinder Naberhaus is a Crystal Kite Award winner and acclaimed author of *Blue Sky White Stars* and *Lines*. She started her career writing songs, at age eight. She was born in India and grew up in the heartland of America.

Lupe Ruiz-Flores is the author of six award-winning bilingual children's picture books and several poems. She currently lives in Texas but has also lived in Bangkok, Thailand, and Okinawa, Japan.

Baptiste Paul is the author of three picture books: *The Field*, *Adventures to School*, and *I Am Farmer*. Born and raised on the Caribbean island of Saint Lucia, Paul is a native Creole/patois speaker. He holds degrees in environmental studies and political science from Bucknell University and currently resides with his family in Green Bay, Wisconsin.

Cynthia Leitich Smith is a *New York Times* best-selling author of fiction for children and young adults. A member of the Muscogee Creek Nation, she writes stories centered on the lives of modern-day American Indians. Her works for young readers include *Holler Loudly, Jingle Dancer*, and *Indian Shoes*.

Patti Richards is the author of two children's nonfiction books about space and several short stories that have been published in *Highlights Magazine* and *Amazon Rapids*. Her picture book, *Dancing Grannies*, was a finalist in the 2014 Katherine Paterson Prize for Young Adult and Children's Writing at Hunger Mountain. Richards lives and writes in Farmington Hills, Michigan.

Chrystal D. Giles is an aspiring author of picture books and middle grade novels. She is a member of the Society of Children's Book Writers and Illustrators, and she was chosen as a 2018 We Need Diverse Books Mentee.

Margarita Engle is the national Young People's Poet Laureate Emeritus. She is a Cuban American author of many verse novels, including *The Surrender Tree*, a Newbery Honor winner. Her verse memoir, *Enchanted Air*, received the Pura Belpré Award and Lee Bennett Hopkins Poetry Award, among others. She lives in central California.

Kenn Nesbitt wrote his first children's poem when he was thirty-two years old. Now he has written more than a dozen books and is a former Children's Poet Laureate, named by the Poetry Foundation. Nesbitt travels around the world inspiring thousands of students each year.

JaNay Brown-Wood is a children's author and educator. Her picture book *Imani's Moon* won the NAESP Children's Book of the Year Award and was a Reading Is Fundamental (RIF) Multicultural Book pick for 2015. Brown-Wood's poetry has been featured in *Highlights* and *High Five*. She lives in Sacramento, California.

Diana Murray immigrated to the United States from Ukraine at age two and became a citizen at age nine. Her picture books include *Ned the Knitting Pirate*, *Grimelda the Very Messy Witch*, and *City Shapes*, a Junior Library Guild Selection. Her poems have appeared in *Highlights*, *High Five*, *Hello, Spider*, *Ladybug*, and other magazines. She lives in New York City.

Megan Hoyt is the daughter of symphony musicians, so she grew up tapping her toes backstage, listening to the dips and swells, beats and rhythms of masterful music. Her first picture book, *Hildegard's Gift*, is a biography of medieval composer Hildegard of Bingen. Hoyt currently lives in Charlotte, North Carolina.

Jamie McGillen holds a BA in English with an emphasis in creative writing from Western Washington University and an MA in English from Northern Arizona University. Her work has been published in *Rust + Moth*, *Marathon Literary Review*, and the *Raven Chronicles*. She is a mom to two children, who both happen to be obsessed with rocks.

Renée M. LaTulippe has coauthored nine early readers, and her poems have been widely published in anthologies for children. She earned her BFA in acting/directing from Marymount Manhattan College and her MA in English education from NYU. LaTulippe teaches writing in her online course the Lyrical Language Lab. She lives by the sea in Italy.

Vanessa Brantley-Newton was born during the civil rights movement and attended school in Newark, New Jersey. She celebrates self-love and acceptance of all cultures through her work, and hopes to inspire young readers to find their own voices—which has earned her the title Spreader of Sunshine. Brantley-Newton is the illustrator of nearly eighty books for children.

Traci Sorell grew up immersed with stories and accounts of her ancestors' lives, which mirrored her Cherokee heritage. She writes poems as well as fiction and nonfiction stories for children and teens. She is the author of two picture books, *We Are Grateful: Otsaliheliga*, featuring the universal spirit of gratitude as experienced through modern Cherokee culture across the four seasons, and *At the Mountain's Base*, a circular story in verse.

Edna Cabcabin Moran is an illustrator who paints, draws, designs, writes, and dances hula. In her youth, she played among boulders in Iceland's tundra, hung out in a bustling Norcal navy town, and bicycled daily through the sprawl of Honolulu. She is author and/or illustrator of four books for children including *The Sleeping Giant: A Tale from Kaua'i*.

Charles "Father Goose" Ghigna lives in a treehouse in the middle of Alabama. He is the author of more than one hundred books and more than five thousand poems for children and adults. Ghigna has read his poems at the Library of Congress, the John F. Kennedy Center for the Performing Arts, and the International Schools of South America.

Liz Garton Scanlon is the author of more than a dozen beloved picture books, including the Caldecott-honored *All the World, Another Way to Climb a Tree*, and *Kate, Who Tamed the Wind*. Scanlon is on the faculty of the Vermont College of Fine Arts and is a frequent presenter at schools and festivals. She lives in Austin, Texas.

Marlena Myles is a Spirit Lake Dakota/Mohegan/Muscokee Creek artist and designer. She uses her art to celebrate her Indigenous culture and language and to help the public understand the significance of Native oral traditions and history.

Editor's Note to Educators and Parents

While my goal in editing this collection was to feature the poets, I'd like to share a few words. Children's books about gratitude are prominently displayed in autumn, but they often lack visibility during other seasons. Giving thanks is something that can and does happen all year long. This sentiment, combined with a passion for poetry and my advocacy for diverse books, sparked the vision for *Thanku*—a collection suitable for any season and filled with diverse formats and voices.

I remember being in school and learning happy lessons about the first Thanksgiving. One autumn, we even made pilgrims and "Indians" out of oatmeal canisters and toilet paper rolls. I wasn't aware that there was much more to the story than what I was taught, or that the assigned activities and my participation in them were misrepresenting, distorting, and shaming other cultures. The myths and half-truths about the history of this feast have damaged the cultural self-esteem of generations of Indigenous people and perpetuated negative images. Presenting Thanksgiving to children primarily as a happy time diminishes our shared history and gives an incomplete account of the diversity among Native and First Nations people. And while elementary-aged children who discuss the first Thanksgiving at school may not be ready to process some of the atrocities, history needs to be taught factually. Educators must examine the inclusivity of their teaching materials as well as their own biases.

Learning and sharing the fuller context of Thanksgiving doesn't mean that we need to stop celebrating entirely. Many citizens of the hundreds of Indigenous Nations within the United States and Canada give thanks to the Creator not once a year, but every day, for all the gifts of life. On Thanksgiving, Americans reach out in significant numbers to people in need within their communities. Might we start there and move forward? While we cannot change the past, we can acknowledge its consequences and work for peace and unity in the future.

Undoubtedly, this collection will land among Thanksgiving-themed displays of books, next to titles with varied historical or cultural takes on the harvesttime holidays. If you're a parent or educator who sets aside time—during any part of the year—to discuss autumn feasting or Indigenous peoples (and I hope you do), I invite you to consult and implement the resources listed below.

In the words of hinmatóowyalahtq'it, also known as Chief Joseph (Nez Perce), "Good words do not last long unless they amount to something."

In Peace and Gratitude,

Miranda Paul

Resources

Barrows, Sally, and Holly Stewart, eds. "American Indian Perspectives on Thanksgiving." National Museum of the American Indian Education Office. Accessed February 27, 2018. https://nmai.si.edu/sites/1/files/pdf/education/thanksgiving_poster.pdf.

"Native Knowledge 360: Framework for Essential Understandings about American Indians." National Museum of the American Indian Education Office. Accessed February 27, 2018. https://si.edu/nk360/about.cshtml.

Reese, Debbie. "Dear Teachers: An Open Letter about Images of Indians." American Indians in Children's Literature. November 17, 2015. https://americanindiansinchildrensliterature.blogspot.com/2015/11/dear-teachers-open-letter-about-images.html.

"Values/Ruth A. Myers Center for Indigenous Education." College of Education and Human Service Professions, University of Minnesota. Accessed February 26, 2019. https://cehsp.d.umn.edu/node/1746.